Cabin Collectibles

Decorated canoe paddles were made from a variety of woods and are often an inexpensive way of adding interesting forms to rustic settings.

CABIN

Collectibles

Written and Photographed by

Ralph Kylloe

GIBBS·SMITH
P
PUBLISHER

Salt Lake City

First Edition
04 03 02 01 00   4 3 2 1

Published by
Gibbs Smith, Publisher
P.O. Box 667
Layton, Utah 84041

Orders: (1-800) 748-5439
E-mail: info@gibbs-smith.com
Website: www.gibbs-smith.com

Edited by Suzanne Taylor
Designed and produced by FORTHGEAR, Inc.
Printed and bound in China

Library of Congress Cataloging-in-Publication Data

Kylloe, Ralph R.
      Cabin collectibles / written and photographed by Ralph Kylloe.
           p. cm.
      ISBN 0-87905-965-6
      1. Decoration and ornament, Rustic. 2. Outdoor life—Collectibles. I. Title.

      NK1986.R8 K95 2000
      745—dc21

                                                                    99-045216

Table of Contents

Acknowledgments

I cannot say thank you enough to the dozens of individuals around the country who have not only been instrumental in letting me photograph their homes and collections as well as sharing information with me but who have also become great friends with my wife and me over the years. I wish to personally thank John and Jo Ann Lefner, Bob Oestreicher, Henry Caldwell, Jeff Cherry, Don Williams, Chris Williams and the Old Hickory Furniture Company, Jack Leadley, Michael and Terry Griffin, Barney Bellinger, Connie and Rich Moore, Hank and Robert Ross, Allan Newell, Diana Beattie, and numerous others whose names elude me at this moment. I must also say a profound thank you to my publisher, Gibbs Smith, and to my editor, Suzanne Taylor. I thank all of you. Finally, I must acknowledge my wife, Michele, and my daughter, Lindsey. Michele runs my business, styles and decorates numerous projects we are involved with, and keeps me in line. My daughter, certainly the thrill of my life, provides more fun for me than I ever thought possible. I just hope she loves rustic furniture as much as I do!

Foreword

For the past two decades I have had the opportunity to be involved in decorating in the rustic style hundreds of homes, retreats, lodges, resorts, camps, cabins, restaurants, taverns, retail stores of all kinds, and numerous other facilities. I have to say that I have the greatest job in the world. Many of these projects have been on the grand scale. For instance, during the summer of 1996 I provided rustic accessories for new clothing stores in Italy. Over a two-month period I collected more than 350 pairs of antique skis and poles, 350 pairs of antique snow-shoes, 200 fishing creels, 250 antique sleds, 200 antique camp signs, hundreds of old bamboo fly rods, and more rustic stuff than I can remember. The entire project was contained in two monstrous forty-foot containers and shipped, to the great satisfaction of the storeowners, to Italy on time!

Because of my experience in the field, I have had the opportunity to study thousands of rustic items and have gained an in-depth understanding of these items. I have also written and photographed seven books (my eighth will be out in fall 2000) and numerous articles on rustic style. In general, the books have focused on rustic furniture, outdoor rustic garden architecture, and related areas of interest. Many of the photographs have contained exceptional collections of rustic accessories, including fishing creels, Adirondack pack baskets, and canoe paddles. Although I have written at length on the history of rustic furniture, I find I am called upon almost daily to provide information on many of the accessories featured in my books.

As a result, I suggested to Gibbs Smith, the publisher of most of my books, that we should do a small book on accessories. Fortunately, he enthusiastically agreed, and I began assembling information.

Do not expect this book to be a price guide to rustic accessories. I have always felt that price guides were less than academic, as prices often quoted were misleading in many of the guides I have seen. Apart from that, the price of an antique in New York City is dramatically different from the same item in northern Wisconsin. As such, the function of this book is to provide a very basic overview containing general information on rustic items that are often used to decorate today's homes.

Realistically, if one is willing to do the research, there are numerous contemporary and historical treatises that offer extensive information on a number of subjects covered in this book. I have listed several of these in the Resources section.

I will be the first to admit that this book is far from complete. It is, however, an attempt to answer very basic questions about only a few of the really great "folk art" rustic items that exist today. Along with touching on a few of the antique items that are presently collected, I have also included a brief look at several exceptional artists presently working today.

As with all bodies of work, there are far more people in the world who have bits and pieces of information that add to a body of knowledge. Individuals are invited to drop me a note with information that may be relevant to the growing interest in "things rustic."

Ralph Kylloe, Ed.D.

This back porch of an Adirondack cabin is decorated in classic rustic style. The chairs were made by the Old Hickory Chair Company of Martinsville, Indiana, around 1910 and are rare because of the extended spindles below the arms. Locally found pack baskets, fishing creels, signs, and thermos bottles adorn the walls. The red blanket is signed with a label that reads "Hudson Bay." The Rustic Hickory Furniture Company of La Porte, Indiana, made the hat rack around 1915.

Human beings have an incredible propensity to collect things. Many of us go to great extremes and expense to have some "little treasures" hanging from our walls or displayed artistically in cabinets. In general, our collections are important only to us as individuals.

One of my first forays into collecting focused on printed images of birds of prey. As a young man, I was a falconer and flew some of these birds for sport. For years I collected hundreds of images of predatory birds found on all sorts of printed material. Unfortunately, during a move to a different state, a friend who was helping me with my travels saw the collection and, thinking the images were worthless, deposited them in a trash bin. To this day I feel that I lost something of great value.

Canoes are often cut in half and used as display shelves. Rustic items such as bait buckets, creels, camp signs, and other collectibles add to the display.

Most other collections, however, are easily recognized for their value and are respected immediately for their uniqueness and individuality. Museums and other places obviously have collections for observation and research.

But of interest to many is why we collect things in the first place. At face value, this is not an easy question to answer. Nonetheless, literature in the fields of psychology, anthropology, and sociology, among others, are replete with discourses on the topic.

At the heart of present-day arguments is the need to ground ourselves to the world. It is argued that collections and souvenirs bring us closer to humanity and remind us of places we have been and events we have attended. Our little treasures serve to bind us together and remind us of shared and personal experiences.

Other arguments on a more practical side also exist. Many collections have been acquired first for enjoyment but have turned into significant investments. Those of us who purchased and kept early Barbie dolls, baseball cards, marbles, Walt Disney memorabilia, early toys of all sorts, Arts & Crafts pottery, Depression glass, Christmas ornaments, Oriental rugs, and other items too numerous to mention are today quite pleased with the financial value of these purchases.

Other arguments indicate that collectibles are needed by us as décor throughout our homes. Sociologists will argue that collections and the arrangements of them throughout our own environments are nothing more than an individual's attempt to control and manipulate this environment.

These arguments certainly offer merit and cannot be dismissed. However, I and countless other passionate collectors throughout the world find that we are driven by intrinsic motivation more than anything else. We dearly love the items we so aggressively seek, and we find absolute joy in the hunt to add one more little treasure to our collections.

On Things Rustic

There is, however, another reason for some of us to be so passionate about certain types of collectibles—one that is far more deeply imbedded in our very nature and fabrics. For hundreds of millions of generations throughout our early human efforts, we lived very close to the land. We were hunters and gatherers. We carried with us our fishing poles. We wore the skins of the animals we hunted. We kept the antlers and skulls of the things we hunted as souvenirs of the hunt. We had our spears and bows and arrows with us, ready for use at all times. We lived in caves and huts, and we painted scenes of our daily activities on the walls of the places where we spent the long nights. In the evenings we sat on primitive chairs made of tree stumps, and sat around fires that kept us warm and drove away beasts that hunted us. We saw great forests and clean rivers, streams, lakes, and oceans. We were a part of nature, not apart from it.

This way of living is hard-wired in us. This is one reason why we keep plants and pets in our homes, vacation in remote areas, and go to the oceans and woods to ponder life's great personal questions.

We have recently become passionate and obsessive about things "rustic." But I must mention that this is not a trend or a fad. Recognition of the inherent uniqueness of rustic collectibles—such as fishing creels and fishing gear, snowshoes and old skis, old camp signs, old canoes and paddles, vintage photographs, birch-bark picture frames, and numerous other rustic cabin accessories—is more of a reawakening of the heritage within us.

When we spend time in a rustic environment such as a cabin in the woods or a ranch on the slopes of a great prairie, we feel rejuvenated, refreshed. Our cares slip away. Problems are less ominous, and we are able to reconnect to things that are deeply personal and important in our lives. The language spoken by humans is woefully inept when it comes to describing these feelings or the beauty of a sunset or the mysteries of things that reside below the surface of the water.

And so we return to our primitive and uniquely human past to rekindle our spirits. It is a part of us that cannot be repressed. Every once in a while we dream of the woods and of the water and of the monsters and beasts that reside there. It is from where we come and to where we always return.

Highly decorated canoes were popular in the 1920s and were offered by a number of canoe companies.

Canoes and Paddles

Canoes and paddles are often included in the décor of rustic settings. Hung upside down from ceilings, canoes of all makes and models offer high drama to any setting. Canoes that have been damaged on one end are often cut in half and made into display cases that become homes to any number of rustic collectibles.

In general, paddles with wide blades were made by coastal Native Americans such as the Micmacs, Penobscots, Malecites, or Passamaquoddys. Craftsmen from interior tribes such as the Cree or Tete De Boule made narrow-bladed paddles, mostly from maple or spruce.

Paddles of all sizes are often hung on walls or displayed prominently in homes around the country. Vintage photos of individuals in canoes are also highly sought by designers and collectors.

Canoes and boats bring us close to the mysteries of nature and remind us of the lazy, hot days of summer; of summer camps and daredevil dives into crystal clear lakes; of fishing with bobbers and worms; of tired muscles after a long day's paddle; and of easy times. They also remind us of the subtle communication between two canoe paddlers and the artistic movements that become a dance as the paddlers propel a canoe through calm waters.

But equally important is that many of the forms used in canoes and paddles are highly expressive art forms themselves. The teardrop shapes of canoe paddles and the graceful, sensual, sweeping lines of canoes carry emotional overtones. The quality of a well-formed paddle

This display includes a high-end collection of one-of-a-kind painted paddles, mostly of Native American origin. The two center paddles are more than seven and a half feet long and were traditionally used as steering paddles in very large canoes, such as war canoes or transportation boats. The pair of armchairs and the table were made of yellow birch in the Adirondacks in the early 1900s. Fishing creels, Old Hickory furniture, and pack baskets provide nostalgic accents.

17

or a birch-bark canoe is easily recognized and is a pleasure to enjoy.

Canoes and paddles of some sort have been with the human race since we first jumped onto a log and realized the necessity of having a tool to propel and guide us across the water. Museums across the world have numerous primitive boats and paddles in their collections that indicate a significant historical connection with our "hunter/gatherer lifestyles."

Paddles and canoes, like all other human endeavors, evolved with regional styles and differences. Today serious collectors can identify individual historical builders, tribes, materials, subtle regional differences, and décor of many different variations. And, of course, the great pieces are very hard to find.

Certainly the earliest North American boats were those made by Native Americans who established styles that were indicative of the regions in which they lived. The earliest documentations of both canoes and paddles were records from French

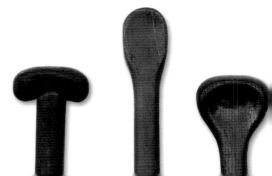

ABOVE: Detail of a paddle painting by Al Keech. FAR LEFT: Paddles with small handles or grips were made by tribes such as the Cree or Algonquins. The center paddle has a traditional small Cree handle and is probably from the early 1800s. NEAR LEFT: Micmacs, Malecites, Algonquins, and other tribes made variations on the forms shown here. The large handle on the left indicates a coastal design.

Penobscot Indians in central Maine made this birch-bark canoe in the late 1890s. It was found hanging in a barn in Vermont. Today it hangs majestically in the Pioneer Saloon in Ketchum, Idaho. The canoe measures seventeen feet ten inches and, with its low-rise bow and stern, is a classic Penobscot design.

explorers in the 1500s. Explorers over the next hundred years were quite amazed at the artistic and engineering accomplishments of both canoe and paddle makers from numerous tribes along the northern regions of America and Canada. Canoe builders from such tribes as Micmac, Malecite, Cree, Tetes de Boule, Montagnais, Algonquin, Ojibway, and others created canoes that were much faster and lighter than anything brought over by the Europeans. And today, historical birch-bark canoes are held in high esteem by a few lucky individuals who can find and afford them.

Canoe paddles are also marvels of design. Shapes of blades and types of handles identify historical paddles. Twentieth-century commercial paddles are also collectible. Many have aged to rich golden colors and are wonderfully painted.

Detail of a riverfront paddle painting by Al Keech.

Color Design No. 4, $18.00

Color Design No. 22, $18.00

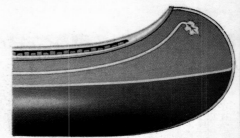
Color Design No. 23, $14.00

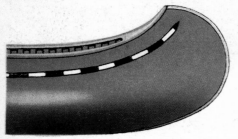
Color Design No. 31, $10.00

Color Design No. 32, $11.00

Color Design No. 16, $9.50

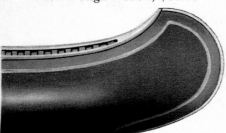
Color Design No. 10, $10.00

Color Design No. 33, $5.50

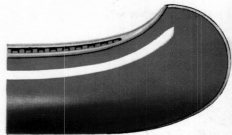
Color Design No. 34, $4.00

COLOR DESIGNS

In these end sections of "OLD TOWN CANOES" is shown a wide range of designs for the whole length of the canoe. In ordering please specify the design number and price as indicated. These designs are susceptible of various color schemes, and can be executed in any combination of colors you may submit. Price of design No. 23 includes mahogany rub rails ($5.00) which separate the colors. Assortment of these designs in stock but suggest allow ten days.

An example of color designs of the Old Town Canoe Company of Old Town, Maine, from its 1929 catalog.

As the Industrial Revolution came into full swing, numerous commercial efforts in Canada and America further established varying designs in canoes and paddles that today are considered collectible. In America, the Charles River section in Boston was known to house at least a dozen canoe manufacturers, including the Waltham Canoe Company, Ted Shea Canoes, J. H. Robertson Canoe Company and numerous others. The Old Town Canoe Company, located in Old Town, Maine, opened its doors in the early part of the century and is still building high-end canoes today. Many of the commercially made canoes were signed and, with some searching, a signature may reveal itself. Old Town canoes are easy to identify. Typically, Old Town used diamond-shaped fasteners on top of the gunwales and thwarts as securing devices. Old Town often etched numbers on the bow floorboards. If you give the numbers to Old

Bow section of an Ojibway canoe from the 1920s.

Detail of a paddle painting by Al Keech.

Town, they will be more than happy to tell you what year the canoe was made.

In Canada, companies such as the Chestnut Canoe Company, Lake Field, William English, Peterborough, Rice Lake, and others flourished for decades. The efforts of individual craftsmen living in remote northern areas established significant definable paddle and canoe styles as well. Guides living in the Adirondacks, Maine, Canada, Minnesota, and other regions created styles that were quite different from the commercially made paddles of the day.

Around the turn of the century, owners of wilderness resorts, camps, and lodges found that many tourists appreciated boats and paddles and wanted something to take home with them. Understandably, local crafters and folk artists produced numerous small souvenirs that could be purchased at

Classical East Coast Native American canoe-paddle handles were often longer and used by the stern paddler to steer large canoes.

This canoe was made by the Chestnut Canoe Company in Canada in the 1930s.
Its small size, twelve feet, allows the canoe to be used decoratively in a variety
of settings. Pack baskets and camp signs make handsome complements.

A collection of small paddles is displayed on a birch-bark rack. The paddles, painted by Al Keech and often signed "Thousand Islands" feature scenes from the St. Lawrence Seaway.

tourist shops by visitors. At the same time, many of these same retail stores were able to purchase large quantities of souvenir goods through wholesale outlets. These same stores then placed decals that indicated the regions visited by the tourists. For instance, it is quite common to find small paddles, miniature canoes, and other related items with decals stating "Adirondack Mountains," "Catskill Mountains," "Appalachian Mountains," and numerous other regions.

Many summer camps for boys and girls offered craft classes for their guests. As projects, campers often decorated camp paddles with colorful designs, names, and dates. It is not uncommon to find paddles that were also adorned with carved scenes of deer, log cabins, mountains, or floral or geometric patterns. Canoe paddles that had patterns "burned" into them can be found occasionally. Various clubs around the country also maintained

Further examples of coastal and interior canoe handles, which often had "steps" cut into the handles; interior handles were usually molded or formed to fit the hands of the various makers.

paddles that had their club logos inscribed on them. Other paddles have been found that were dated and signed by numerous individuals who had experienced a lengthy wilderness trip together.

Along with the above efforts, artists with significant abilities were also known to decorate paddles. A. F. Tate, whose work resides in museums around the country, was a summer resident in the Adirondacks in the 1860s and was known to paint scenes on paddles and present them as gifts to friends.

Another individual, Al Keech, a lifelong resident of the Thousand Island region along the St. Lawrence River in New York, created wonderful small tourist-trade paddles that he personally hand painted with scenes from the northern Adirondack region. Keech was a writer, commentator, and painter. His

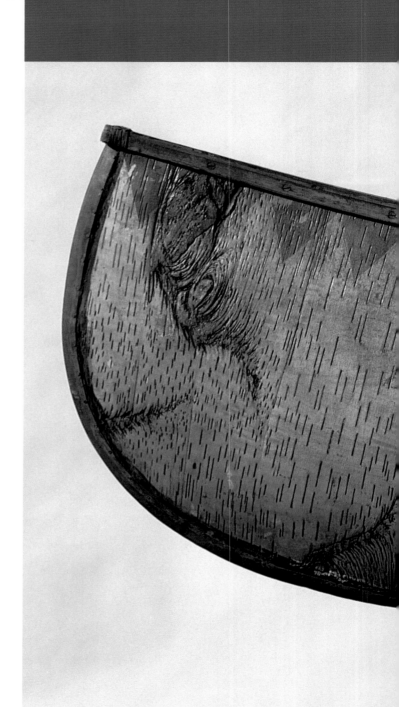

The cover from Old Town Canoe Company's 1929 catalog.

painted paddles, unmistakable to collectors familiar with his work, were usually twenty-two inches long and made of softwoods. Of the 150 or so known paddles he made, none have been found with his signature. Keech died in 1926. His paddles are highly sought after and have appreciated dramatically over the past few years.

The "mother of all paddles," however, is the one made of bird's-eye maple. Much sought after by collectors, paddles made of this material are prized and prominently displayed by their proud owners. Different makers throughout the northern region made bird's-eye paddles, so many different styles exist.

Decals, like the one on the blade of this canoe paddle found in northern Maine, came from regions across the country and were manufactured by several different companies and sold to entrepreneurs, who then placed them on their products.

This collection of Native American–made collectibles is indicative of those that were often made for the tourist trade. Such items are typically displayed in groups.

Snowshoes

Like many other tools necessary for survival, snowshoes have been with the human race for the past several millennia. The earliest recorded snowshoes date to around 6,000 years ago.

Used by humans all across the northern belt of the earth, snowshoes allowed their users to transport themselves throughout the frozen tundra regions.

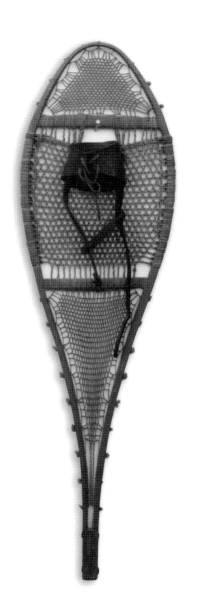

Today numerous snowshoe companies exist and find a thriving market for their wares. While today's hi-tech world has applied all its resources to create snowshoes of such materials as PVC, aluminum, nylon, and others, numerous folk artists across North America have struggled to reinstate the almost-lost art of snowshoe making. This will only increase as the public becomes aware of the beauty and grace of handmade Indian snowshoes.

The most-prized snowshoes are those that were handmade by Native cultures all across the northern regions of this country. In the Northeast, snowshoes were made by such culturally rich tribes as the Attikamek, Cree, Algonquin, Micmac, Penobscot, Malecite, and

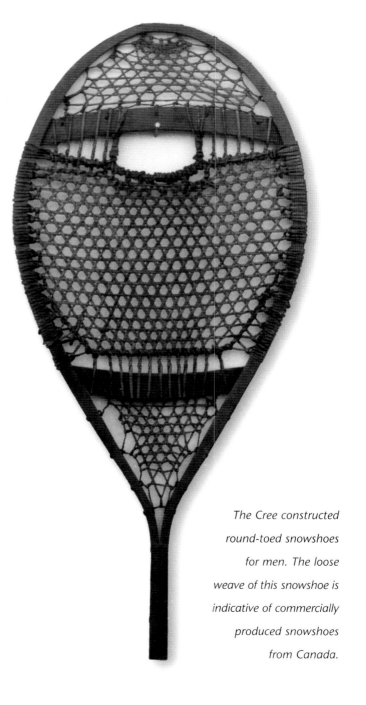

The Cree constructed round-toed snowshoes for men. The loose weave of this snowshoe is indicative of commercially produced snowshoes from Canada.

Abenaki. Today many examples of Native-made snow-shoes hold honorable places in museums and are the object of study and affection for admirers.

The most complete work on making snowshoes is a wonderful book written by Henri Vaillancourt. *Making the Attikamek Snowshoe* was published by the Trust for Native American Cultures and Crafts and offers the reader an in-depth look at the historical and artistic perspectives of a craft that was almost lost to the ravages of technology and time.

Snowshoes come in a variety of shapes and sizes. Long narrow snowshoes are referred to as Michigans or pickerels. Those longer than they are wide are generally used in open fields and are considered more stable. Snowshoes that are very wide and almost circular are called bear paws and are generally used in densely wooded areas as well as in hilly terrain.

Different snowshoes were also designed and constructed for various snow conditions. When the snow was light and powdery, snowshoes that had a very tight mesh prevented snow from passing through. Snowshoes for

A unique pair of "tear-drop" snowshoes hand-made by Native Americans in the early part of the twentieth century. Tightness of the weave is indicative of high quality.

Classical oversized snowshoes made by Native Americans; notice the weaving, which does not extend around the outer frame of the snowshoe. Such examples are referred to as "spring" snowshoes. Tightness of the weave, as well as their condition, make these snowshoes very collectible.

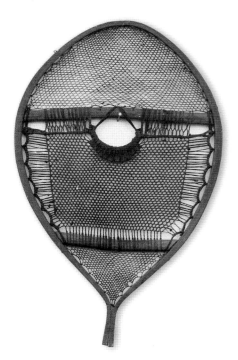

frozen crusty snow were usually smaller and maintained a more open weave.

Further, different seasons called for different snowshoe designs. Winter snowshoes were made by wrapping the woven material completely around the outer frame of the snowshoe. Users found that winter snow was less abrasive on the woven material, which also added a bit of extra traction in the snow. Nonetheless, occasionally the outer edges of the winter snowshoes were covered with a skin or canvas to protect the weaving from possible damage. Spring snowshoes were constructed by attaching the material to an inner selvage cord, thus leaving the wooden frame exposed to the immediate elements.

Traditionally, there was also a difference between men's and women's snowshoes.

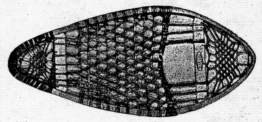

Bean's Bear Paw Snowshoes

Made from the same fine grain State of Maine ash that we use on our Maine Snowshoes on opposite page. The filling will not sag.

This type is very popular with guides, lumber cruisers and trappers who are obliged to travel in thick growth.

Size 14 x 30. Price $7.50 postpaid.

Bean's Hickory Skis

This is the second year we have listed Skis. Our selection is the result of ski experts' opinions as to a suitable Ski for both professional and amateur. Carefully milled from selected Southern Hickory.

Price, length 6¾ ft. Ridge top as shown above $8.75.
Length 6½ ft. and 6¾ ft. Flat top as shown below $5.75.

We recommend the 6½ ft. Flat top for Ladies. Postpaid East of Mississippi, if West add 50¢.

Bean's Improved Snow-shoe Rigging

Made from a heavy, pliable oil tanned leather. The construction is simple yet practical.

Similar to our 1935 Sandal but much more effective. It gives the wearer absolute control.

Price $1.15 postpaid.

Summer Care of Snow-shoes

Wipe clean and varnish both the wood and webbing. Any high grade spar varnish will do. Two coats are better than one but in any case they should be thin coats.

Tie the Shoes securely together, back to back, and force block of wood into the space between the toes.

Place them out of the sun and hang by the tail. Suspend by wire so that mice or squirrels cannot get at them.

L. L. BEAN INC. FREEPORT MAINE

This office setting includes an extremely rare desk made by the Old Hickory Chair Company around 1910. The pair of oval snow-shoes are also rare and were probably made by the Attikamek Indians in the early 1900s. The outer pair of snowshoes are of the same vintage. Both pairs still boast their original caribou-skin weaving.

Men's snowshoes tended to be larger than women's. Small snowshoes were also made for children. Further, certain tribes, including the Manouane, earmarked square-toed snowshoes for women and round-toed snowshoes for men. In the past, women's and sometimes children's snowshoes were adorned with ribbons or other materials.

Many tribes also decorated snowshoes. Vaillancourt describes four ways of decoration or embellishment:

1. applying tufts of colored yarn on the outside of the frames;
2. weaving a geometric pattern into the material;
3. painting each area of the snowshoe with different colors; or,
4. hollowing out the toe section of the frame.

Snowshoes have been made with different woods, including yellow birch, white birch, black ash, and maple. Material used for the woven areas has traditionally been caribou skin. Today, however, moose skin, which is not as pliable as caribou, is used as material for weaving.

These square-toed shoes were often designated by the Cree as women's snowshoes. Because the woven material extends around and outside the outer frame, they were called "winter" snowshoes.

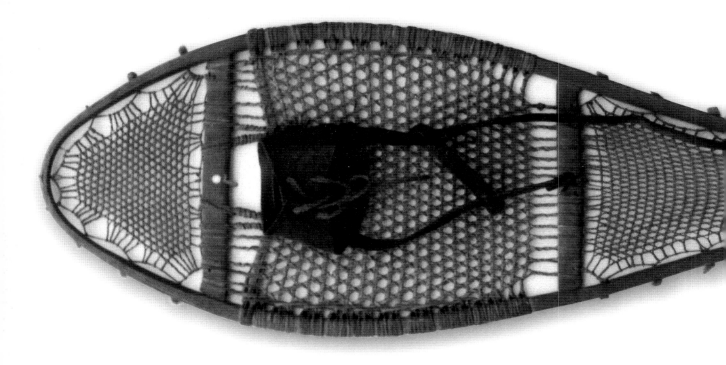

The beauty of Native American snowshoes is immediately recognizable. Stitching on high-quality snowshoes is often tighter than six knots per inch. Many of the older vintage snowshoes have mellowed to rich colors. Collectors prize quality examples of Native American snowshoes and often go to great effort and expense to enhance their collections.

During the Industrial Revolution, numerous commercial efforts benefited by mass-producing snowshoes based on designs initiated and developed by Native American cultures. Many of the names that carried snowshoes in the early part of the twentieth century were companies such as L. L. Bean of Maine, David T. Abercrombie Co. of New York City, Sears, Roebuck & Co. of Chicago, and others. Realistically, such catalog companies simply purchased snowshoes and

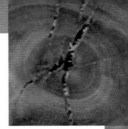

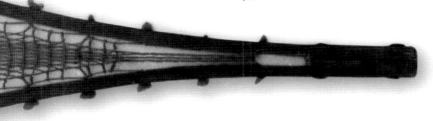

Leather bindings or simple straps secured snowshoes to the feet. When adorned with tufts of colored fabric along the outer edge of the frame, these winter snowshoes were usually, but not always, made for women and children.

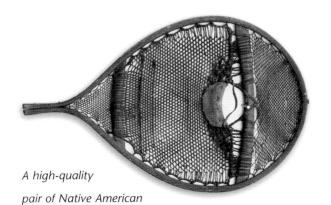

A high-quality pair of Native American spring snowshoes.

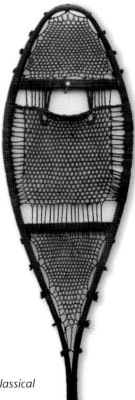

A high-quality collectible snowshoe with a classical square pattern woven into the center section.

This is a classical example of "pickerel," or "Michigan," snowshoes. They are made of ash and strung with rawhide. Long snowshoes such as these were frequently used on open prairies and flatlands.

other equipment from manufacturers around the country and then placed their names on the products. At the same time, L. L. Bean was known to employ Native Americans to make many of their products, including snowshoes.

W. F. Tubbs Company of Norway, Maine, opened its doors around 1905 and made snowshoes of ash for many years. Their products are easily identifiable today by observing a brand or a metal plate fixed to the center of the snowshoe. Tubbs also manufactured high-quality skis, snowshoe riggings, and ski poles. In the early part of the 1900s, other manufacturers, such as the Lund Snowshoe Company of Minnesota, the Strand Ski Co. of New Richmond, Wisconsin (which made skis of hickory), the Northland Ski Mfg. Company of St. Paul, Minnesota, and the W. H. Ketchum Company of Gaysville, Vermont, manufactured high-quality products that are often collected today.

Human beings have an incredible propensity to collect things. Many of us go to great extremes and expense to have some little treasures hanging from our walls or displayed artistically in cabinets. In general, our collections are important only to us as individuals.

The Maine Snow-shoe

If there is a better Snow-Shoe made we certainly would like to see it. The frames are especially selected State of Maine second growth white ash butts, seasoned so they will not warp. The filling is the very best cowhide, cured by a secret process that positively prevents sagging. The workmanship is so well done that it gives the shoe a perfect balance.

Both Men's and Ladies' are very sporty looking shoes. Wool tassels 60¢ extra. Initials on toe bar 60¢ extra. Regular orders filled same day received. With initials or tassels one week.

We recommend sizes as follows:

Men weighing 115 to 140, 12 x 48   Ladies weighing 80 to 120, 12 x 42
Men weighing 140 to 165, 13 x 48   Ladies weighing 120 to 160, 12 x 44
Men weighing 165 to 225, 14 x 48   Price Men's $7.70; Ladies $7.60. Delivered free.

The Pickerel

This new narrow shoe is made of the same high grade material used in the "Maine" Snow-Shoe as shown above.

This type of shoe had its origin in the far North where the Indians needed a light easy running shoe to track down their game on light drifting snow. Beginners can start right off in confidence for the narrow tread and high upturn eliminates interference and tripping.

It does not load and its bearing value is equal to other type of shoes 50% wider.

Note the special rawhide reinforcements at toe and around bars.

Filled with fine mesh in toe and heel and heavy coarse mesh in body.

Three sizes: 9" x 50", 9" x 56", and 10" x 56". Price $8.85 delivered.

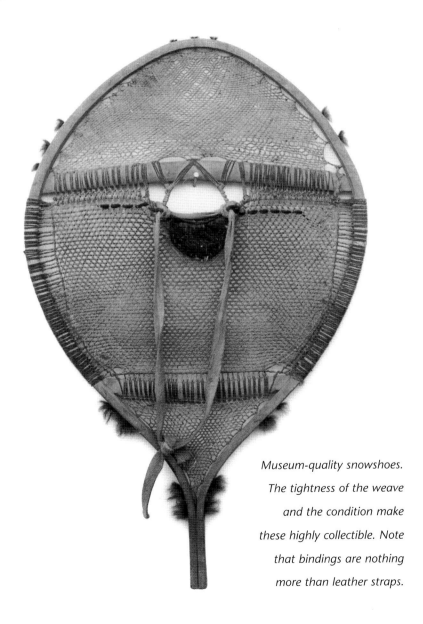

Museum-quality snowshoes. The tightness of the weave and the condition make these highly collectible. Note that bindings are nothing more than leather straps.

Collections of snowshoes are often displayed on walls and above fireplaces. Miniature snowshoes made by Native Americans and sold to the tourist trade around the country are also quite collectible. In the Christmas 1998 issue of *Country Living* magazine, my home was featured. My wife and I had decorated our tree with miniature snowshoes collected over many years. Once the issue hit the stands we received more than a thousand calls from people wanting to know if we would sell some of our miniature snowshoes. Needless to say, we did not sell any of our collection.

Many of the same companies presented

in the previous chapter also manufac-

tured skis and ski poles. Certainly the

innovators of the ski movement were the

Scandinavians, who had acclimated to

the harsh northern climates by creating

various methods of transportation

suitable for their area.

Skis were initially made of old barrel staves and strapped to the skier's feet with leather thongs. This method of binding apparently sufficed for many years. And, no doubt, many a skier spent time recuperating, as such bindings are often referred to today as "ankle-breaker bindings."

Early skis were often made of whatever wood was left after a construction project was finished, of both soft- and hardwoods. The tips of early skis were boiled and bent into whatever shape suited the maker. As the years passed, early-twentieth-century skis were usually made of ash, and later, hickory, and spring-cable bindings were added to provide a safer method of attaching skis to skiers.

Two pairs of early-twentieth-century skis of Scandinavian descent. Both are made of pine and have unusual tips.

A skier in typical 1930s attire, with bamboo poles, square-toed ski boots, and wood-tipped skis.

49

In the 1930s the public was introduced to metal spring bindings; two different examples are shown here.

Pre-1930s skis were often fastened to the skier with leather straps. Both spring-loaded and leather straps are often casually referred to as "ankle-breaker" bindings.

Skis, of course, came in all lengths and widths, for the smallest of children and the largest of adults. The longest pair I have ever found measured an extraordinary nine and a half feet long and almost four inches wide. The bindings on these skis were nothing more than leather straps. Skis this long were used for jumping, while shorter, narrower skis were used for cross-country and downhill skiing.

When skiing first came to the New World, skiers used only one pole. Many of these were made of ash and other hardwoods. In later times, bamboo was used so that when the poles broke under extreme pressure, they would not cause serious injury to skiers falling on them.

Wood-tipped skis are earlier than skis with no tips on them. Skis were made by any number of manufacturers, including Lund and Northland Ski Company.

Early commercial skis were not adorned with wooden tips, as shown in this photo.

Tips were later added to commercially made skis with the thought that they would break through the snow easier. Skis during this period were usually made of either hickory or ash.

This collection of rustic accessories, including pack baskets, fishing creels, and birch-bark items, complements the small canoes here, which were often made by Native Americans and sold to the tourist trade.

Adirondack Pack Baskets

Since hikers, explorers, campers, hunters,

and fishermen who trekked the wilds needed

something in which to carry their gear, someone

A well-formed Adirondack or North Woods pack basket, complete with original canvas straps, is probably from the 1930s. Note that the upper rim of the basket is not woven.

many years ago came up with the convenient

idea of strapping a basket on one's back. In

reality, the evolution of pack baskets is nearly

impossible to trace. I have found a few early

A tall pack basket with woven upper rim and original adjustable canvas straps. These baskets were usually made from black ash.

baskets that were signed, but it is unknown whether it was by the person who made it or the person who owned it. I have reviewed an extensive archive of early related photos, and in several dating between the 1880s and 1910, individuals are shown wearing pack baskets.

At the same time, the spring 1937 L. L. Bean catalog offers "Bean's Pack Basket" for $3.90. The advertisement for the basket reads "manufactured . . . by a Tribe of State of Maine Indians who have earned their living by basket making for the last century." This ad suggests that Native Americans may have been making such baskets for the past hundred years. The ad is repeated in at least five Bean catalogs between 1935 and 1940.

L. L. Bean, being the ultimate entrepreneur, also offered a canvas-covered version of the same

A rare and unusual pack, this tightly woven basket has an original wooden bottom and canvas straps.

A "boxy" pack with original leather straps.

A tall, well-formed pack with leather straps and a woven cover, probably from the early 1900s.

pack for an extra sixty cents. The function of the canvas cover was to offer waterproofing to the items carried in the pack. On several occasions I have found packs covered with canvas. A label sewn on the canvas reads "L. L. Bean, Freeport, Maine."

What we do know is that people living in the wilderness areas of the North had very few possessions and very few resources. With necessity demanding a solution, these hardy woodsmen made not only their furniture from what they found in their backyards but their pack baskets as well.

Pack baskets were always made from black ash. Ash trees were cut, pounded, and layered into thin strips. The strips were soaked until pliable, then formed and woven into baskets that met the needs of the builder. Early baskets had straps

These Adirondack pack baskets have been used throughout the northern regions of America for centuries. Traditionally for carrying supplies and equipment, they were first made by Native Americans and sold or traded to settlers. Pack baskets were often painted red to ensure that other hunters did not shoot the individual carrying the basket. The contemporary lamp was made of yellow birch and the antique table was made by the Old Hickory Furniture Company in the 1930s.

The unusually narrow opening and excellent condition of this pack make it very collectible. It is signed on the bottom: "Albert J. Nicola, Enfield, Maine, Genuine Penobscot Indian Baskets."

made of leather, most often from old leather harnesses used on farm animals. When canvas became available in the 1930s, packs that were promoted through catalogs were adorned with canvas straps.

Packs are wonderfully collectible and can carry great stories. I bought a pack recently that had two holes in it. The elderly owner mentioned that he had purchased the pack in the 1930s and had worn it on his first deer-hunting trip. Toward the evening he heard a shot and was thrown to the ground. Moments later he looked up and found that someone had shot at him and struck his basket instead. Shaken, the man found his way home and immediately painted his basket

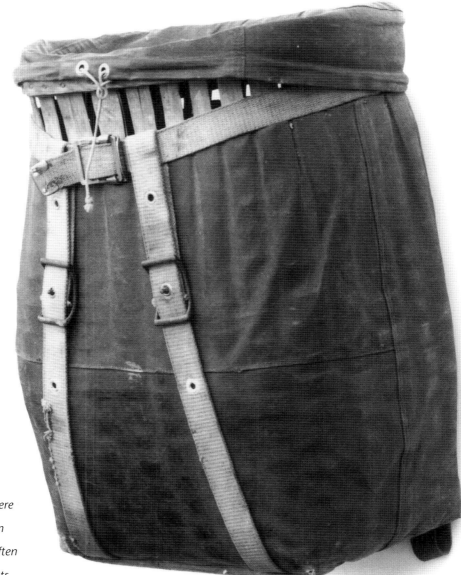

This pack, which has a full canvas covering, is signed "L. L. Bean, Freeport, Maine." Such packs were sold by the company in the 1930s and were often made by the Penobscots and Micmacs.

This cut canoe houses numerous rustic accessories and is ideally suited for corners in homes seeking rustic ambiance. Colorful pack baskets act as accents.

Probably made in the 1930s, this basket has an original plywood top and adjustable leather straps.

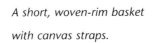

A short, woven-rim basket with canvas straps.

This large basket is complete with original leather straps and handle. It retains its original red paint, which has mellowed to a dark rich patina.

bright red to dissuade hunters from taking further shots at him. He was so shaken by the experience that he never went into the woods again during hunting season. Today his bright red basket, which has mellowed to a dark rich luster, proudly hangs in my study!

The majority of baskets found today are almost rectangular in shape. The very early ones, however, and those that are highly sought after by collectors, are bulbous in form. Collectors occasionally refer to these as "pot-belly" baskets. Their curved lines are exaggerated and are immediately recognizable as unique in form. These antique baskets often have old leather

Pot-belly, or bulbous baskets, are the most collectible of the early varieties.

straps and occasionally have a strand of woven material outlining the edge of the upper rim.

Baskets are often found that are missing a few pieces of weaving. I often purchase old, badly damaged baskets at flea markets for very little money. From these I salvage pieces and weave the material into other baskets that need a little help.

High-end baskets are proudly displayed in collections or as solitary objects of art. Baskets of lesser quality are often used imaginatively as holders for dried flowers, refuse, or laundry.

A traditional pack basket with full woven upper rim, handle, and canvas straps.

A tall pack basket made of ash, often used for ice fishing. They can be found in garages and old barns, complete with ice-fishing tip-ups and ice strainers.

The straps on this pack basket with woven rim have been replaced with shoelaces.

A collection of fishing creels displayed on a North Wing rack.

Fishing creels have become hot items in rustic accessories. Pursued passionately by collectors, creels are now included in almost all collections of rustic accessories.

The Art of the Creel, published by Blue Heron publications in 1997, is considered the bible for those interested in the subject.

This tightly woven "French weave" basket was made in Asia and imported to America.

The earliest records of creels date to the mid-1600s, when creels started showing up in sporting publications in England. At its simplest definition, a creel is a basket that holds fish. Throughout recorded history, creels have been made from many types of materials, including ash, oak, birch, birch bark, willow, wicker, rattan, bamboo, metal, and leather. In America, creels were brought over from England and were eventually imported by the tens of thousands from Japan, China, and Korea.

The real treasures in the antique-creel business, however, are those that were handmade either by Native Americans living all across North America or by a handful of leather workers who lived predominately on the West Coast. Perhaps most beautiful are the imbricated creels (those with overlapping patterns) made of local materials by Native Americans, including the Haida and

A classic, handmade, center-hole, eastern-woodland (Maine) creel made from ash splint.

A classical example of a Japanese splint creel.

Sporting a classical center hole, this handmade wood-splint creel is from the early 1900s.

Tlingit as well as other tribes living in the Northwest. At the same time, the Apache, Navajo, and others of the Southwest also made stunning creels with intricate patterns.

On the East Coast the Iroquois, Micmac, Penobscot, Chippewa, Algonquin, and others produced what have become known as Eastern Woodland creels. These were creels made in an over-and-under weave, checkerboard fashion, out of indigenous materials such as ash, oak, and birch bark.

During the early part of the twentieth century, entrepreneurs began to import creels made in French-weave designs (baskets that are very tightly woven). Baskets that have a loose appearance are called "whole wicker" and were made of both wicker and rattan.

Artist Mark Catman made this collection of contemporary birch-bark creels and baskets. The table was made by John Bennett. The child-sized snowshoes from the 1940s were most likely made by members of the Cree tribe.

A collection of fishing creels rests on a shelf.
Creels were often painted to preserve them.

In America many of the creels were purchased by leather crafters who sewed leather into the creels, thus making them stronger and more durable. Regarded as the finest makers of leather-decorated creels, the George Lawrence Co. of Portland, Oregon, originally manufactured harnesses and saddles. In time the company began producing the most intricate of the leather-reinforced creels. Between the mid-1920s and the mid-1950s, numerous styles were offered to the public through catalogs. Today George Lawrence creels are very rare and bitterly fought over at auctions.

Other leather-bound creels are also on the "hot list." The W. H. McMonies Company, John Clark Saddlery Company, and E. P. Peters Company are also important names associated with high-end creels. The four companies listed here all attached their logos to their products at varying places. Keep in mind that creels were not the sole products of these firms. Rather, they were typically

An early Japanese "French weave" creel; two canvas pockets have been sewn into the lid.

An early, center-hole, eastern-woodland creel from Maine.

involved in the leather/saddlery and harness business and made creels as part of their product lines.

Turtle creels should also be mentioned in the list of high-end creels. Signed "Ilhan New, Boulder, Colo.," these creels had a carved wooden turtle that acted as a securing device. The creels themselves were actually made in Japan or Korea and were embellished here in America.

Early creels generally had a center hole woven into the lid of the creel. As time progressed, holes were offset on the lids. If one was right-handed, then the hole was on the left; the hole was on the right for left-handers.

The earliest record I have found of commercial catalog companies offering creels is the 1917 Sears, Roebuck & Co. catalog, which offered a French willow creel for $1.30. Others, including Abercrombie and L. L. Bean, offered creels in their catalogs in the 1930s.

A handmade ash-splint creel with a "holeless" top and leather tie-down and strap. The creel is signed "A. L." in old paint.

A collection of fishing nets and creels hangs on the walls of this Maine apartment.

A classic eastern-woodlands splint creel found in Maine; it is consistent with early creels made by the Penobscots and Micmacs.

Fishing Nets

Nets of all sorts have been used by humans for centuries and were initially woven together with materials such as grass, animal hair, or vines. In recent years, nets have become symbolic with wilderness-fishing experiences and the outdoors in general. Today many of the early net forms are appreciated for their graceful sweeping curves. Hung on walls, nets offer a rich visual display that will complement any rustic setting.

BASKET AND HARNESS
$1.50 Postpaid

Bean's Fish Basket

Made from finest grade imported white split willow in new form fitting concave back as shown at right. Less bulky than old standard shape.

Size 13″ long on bottom. Price 90¢. Price with solid leather harness designed so that Basket can be worn at side or on back $1.50. Harness only, 65¢ postpaid.

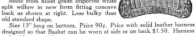

Rooms are often decorated with a variety of cabin collectibles, as shown here. The Indian head was made in the early 1920s and was the figurehead for a boys camp in Maine.

Camp signs add life and humor to any rustic setting. They remind us of our favorite experiences at summer camp or a wonderful weekend with a loved one at a resort. Early signs were painted on wood, and, later, they were often painted or stenciled on metal. Signs were occasionally

made of birch bark that was layed out over boards. Letters were then made of small twigs and nailed onto the birch bark.

Camp signs also come with great names such as "Wa ne lo na" or "Camp We Goofed" or "OMYGOD" or "Camp Whole Lee Kow." Signs of all sorts are fun. The more colorful the better, and if the sign has paintings of buildings, animals, or landscapes it becomes infinitely more interesting.

This contemporary dining-room setting is greatly enhanced by a wall of antique camp signs. The chairs were designed by the author and are manufactured by the Old Hickory Furniture Company of Shelbyville, Indiana. The contemporary burl lamp is classic western style. Creels and canoe paddles complete the setting.

A four-foot cutout sign in old-gold and red paint

found at a flea market in Massachusetts.

This two-sided, wooden shield sign with a pine-tree logo was purchased at an auction in upstate New York.

A study area is made more interesting by the inclusion of old camp signs. The contemporary desk was made with yellow birch legs, a cherry top, and birch siding. The chandelier was constructed with fallow deer antlers. The lamp was made by the Old Hickory Furniture Company. The chair was made at the Indiana State Prison in the 1940s.

This two-sided, black-and-white wooden sign was found in New Hampshire.

Indicative of signs all over the country for camping and RV parks, this single-sided tin sign is eight feet long and presently resides on the side of the author's garage.

The front porch of this log cabin is the site of a collection of antique outboard motors, old camp signs, Old Hickory furniture, creels, nets, waders, and other rustic collectibles.

Birch-bark frames and numerous other bark items were made by various Indian craftsmen from Maine to Minnesota and sold to the tourist trade. To secure the bark together, sweetgrass was woven into the outer edges of the frames.

Birch-Bark Collectibles

Birch trees grow all across North America and their wood makes ideal material for artists and crafters. Long before the arrival of Europeans, Native Americans used the material to make baskets of all sorts as well as canoes and other items. To fill the growing demand for souvenir items, Native Americans fashioned

Frames such as this ten-inch birch-bark item were made by any number of Native American commercial enterprises and sold to tourist shops around the country. They are sewn together with sweet grass.

small canoes, containers of all shapes and sizes, tie racks, picture frames, and numerous other trinkets that could be purchased and carried home by visitors to wilderness areas.

There were different levels of birch-bark collectibles. The inexpensive items were generally plain, while the more expensive things were adorned with intricate decorations, including beads and/or porcupine quills woven into the structure. Beads were generally brought from Italy and traded to the Native Americans. Porcupine quills were harvested by throwing a blanket over a live porcupine, causing it to shoot its quills into the blanket. After the animal found its way to freedom, the

Found in Maine, this small tourist-trade frame with Native American-related postcard is part of the author's collection of more than five hundred such frames.

Many frames were decorated with other organic materials, including walnut shells, funguses, acorns, and antlers. This small frame is adorned with pinecones.

This classical birch-bark frame was made by using the reverse side of the bark as the outer layer. Such frames with their original price tags of ten cents turn up periodically.

blanket was retrieved and the quills that stuck to the blanket were then harvested and used as decorative material on any number of items.

Different centers throughout the North, which were located mostly on Native American reservations, manufactured numerous birch-bark items. Completed goods were then sold wholesale to regional retail stores across the country. Two of the better-known and most-prolific centers were located in Quebec and the Wisconsin Dells.

This highly ornate and intricate frame, found in upstate New York, originally sold for fifteen cents.

Occasionally one finds frames with attached canoes.

This hand-carved, hand-painted wooden fish was made by Lawrence Irvine of Winthrop, Maine, in the late 1960s.

Native Americans made dozens of variations of this bark horseshoe frame.

Brown
St. Paul

Camp Photos

There is something wonderful about a collection

of camp photos. This type of accessory includes

photos of people holding fish, people in canoes or

around campfires, people sitting on the porches

of log cabins, and mountains, trees, and all kinds

of other subjects related to the outdoors. These

are fun things to collect because the subject matter

This photo of a woman in an ornate canoe was probably taken in the 1920s.

is lighthearted in nature and quite fascinating. Look for good contrast and original frames. Avoid water stains and faded images.

An 1880s Adirondack photo with complete camping gear, including Adirondack guide boats, canoe paddles and oars, pack baskets, and freshly caught fish.

Photo of the work yard of the Monohon
Boat/Canoe Company. This company built
high-end boats and was located on the
Charles River in Boston, Massachusetts.

A classic photo of college
teams racing "war" canoes
on the Charles River.

A photo dated February 22, 1906, shows
a group of hardy adventurers preparing
for a winter snowshoe hike.

This mantel is home to a collection of toy furniture made by the Old Hickory Furniture Company between the 1920s and 1940s. Although thought of as "salesmen's samples," they were sold through catalogs as toys for "kids and grown-ups alike." The second-to-last chair on the left was made in Virginia in the 1930s. It was constructed of either rhododendron or mountain-laurel branches.

Rustic Furniture

There is something both earthy and mysterious about rustic furniture. No attempt has been made to hide or disguise the fact that it's made from real wood. All the knots, knobs, gnarls, bumps, twists, turns, bends, and bark are left on the piece. It's completely honest furniture. It's as nature intended it to be—genuinely fun stuff

This toy settee was made from either mountain laurel or rhododendron branches in the 1920s or 1930s. These toys were often made in the Appalachian Mountain range and sold at tourist stores throughout that region.

that has been around a long time. The first piece was made when our early ancestors turned over a log, knocked off a few branches, and sat down to enjoy the evening sunset.

In time, different styles came into being. Based on materials found in their backyards, craftsmen created regional styles that are quite recognizable today. But Americans cannot claim sole ownership of rustic furniture. In truth, rustic furniture is a worldwide phenomenon. Wood-block prints from the fifteenth century show massive tables and chairs made of roots and branches. Important pieces have also been found in France, England, Scotland, Scandinavia, Italy, and many other areas around the world.

Nonetheless, Americans developed their own styles, the most prominent of which is the Adirondack style. Furniture similar to that made in

This setting contains contemporary furniture made by the Old Hickory Furniture Company of Shelbyville, Indiana, as well as several handmade vintage fishing creels, snowshoes, and signs.

the Adirondacks has been found all across the northern states from Maine to Minnesota. This North Woods style, as it should be called, is characterized by birch bark overlaid onto dimensional pieces of furniture, with tiny twigs applied in intricate designs. Some Adirondack pieces were made of cedar and various woods that grow abundantly in the northern regions.

Other regions of the country also saw style developments. In the West, a significant "cowboy" style developed that incorporated Indian motifs into furniture made of lodgepole pine trees and burls. The South saw furniture made from and adorned with roots and branches of both rhododendron and mountain laurel bushes.

The real "shakers and movers" of the rustic furniture business were ten different manufacturers in Indiana. Beginning in the late 1890s these companies produced strong, sturdy furniture made from hickory trees, which were abundant in their area. Certainly the largest, most prolific, and most influential was the Old Hickory Furniture Company of Martinsville, Indiana, which still produces very high-quality furniture today at a new plant in nearby Shelbyville, Indiana. At its peak production, the Old Hickory Furniture Company produced more than 2,000 pieces of rugged handmade furniture a week.

Many major facilities around the country today still use furniture made by the Old Hickory Furniture Company, including the Old Faithful

Inn in Yellowstone National Park and literally thousands of other historical parks, lodges, restaurants, and private homes around the country.

Of significance to the collector is that there are still many early hickory pieces around that can be purchased at reasonable prices. Rustic furniture from Indiana is uniquely American and is today quite functional and stylish. Hickory is the strongest and hardest wood in North America, and furniture made of this material will last, with reasonable care, for centuries.

A few notes on rustic furniture are in order. First, and most importantly, these pieces do not fare well outside. Exposure to rain and sun will ruin a finish and destroy a piece in a few years. A covered porch is okay but do not let them get wet. Pieces of Indiana hickory furniture that are weathered and gray can be brought back to life. On a sunny day, outside, soak them first

In the 1920s, the Old Hickory Furniture Company manufactured and sold doll-size replicas of their furniture in a box that came with a settee, armchair, rocker, and table. They were not sold as salesmen's samples, as is commonly thought.

Contemporary birch-bark shelves provide a home for miniature pieces of rustic furniture and a canoe. The twig stands are native to the East Coast and were made to display photographs.

with water and then apply several coats of a wood or deck cleaner. These products contain a bleaching agent that will return gray pieces to natural colors. Once the chairs are completely dry, sand off any rough edges and then apply a few coats of satin polyurethane or other sealing agent, available at hardware stores.

Woven seats and backs of many older chairs may also be replaced. This is easier to do than one thinks. Materials and how-to books are available at most craft stores. It really takes only a few hours to re-weave a seat, and it is a nice skill to have. Once in a while, you may find an old chair that has been in a barn for many years. Such a chair may have nasty little creatures called powder-post beetles living in them. Watch for small mounds of sawdust that may accumulate under a chair. The best way to treat them is to spray the area and the hole where the sawdust is coming from with either a commercially made insecticide or WD-40. This stuff will penetrate the area and kill almost anything chewing on your treasure.

A word of caution: Once you realize you have these pests, put the chair outside immediately; you do not want these creatures to infest any of your other furnishings.

This display features a most-impressive collection of high-end wooden duck decoys. Its owner spends his spare time rummaging through sales, antiques shops, and flea markets. Birds in mint condition that are well designed and retain original paint often go for tens of thousands of dollars at auctions.

Collectors, myself included, fall into the obsessive/compulsive category. Most of us are a little nuts, but in a positive way. My mother still yells at me, "Fifteen years of college and you sell stick furniture for a living." Fortunately, I, and millions of others like me, pose no threat to society. I love what I do. I often get up at three in the morning

This inlaid, or mosaic, picture frame is part of a three-piece set, probably made in the 1920s. It was found in the Lake George region of Adirondack Park in upstate New York.

and drive to a flea market hundreds of miles away, only to return late that night with nothing to show except a few gas slips and fast-food wrappers in the back seat of my car. I love the things I collect. It's in my blood. I can't help myself. It's as simple as that.

But I've learned many things in the past two decades. The first and most important is to buy only great stuff. In the antiques business, condition is everything. Great pieces will forever go up in value. If you're trying to decorate a house or lodge or whatever, buy only a few great things and you will forever treasure them. You don't need to fill every last inch of your house with stuff.

Game birds such as this one were sold in the 1950s at retail stores around the country. They were hand-painted and are an inexpensive alternative to the classic hand-carved decoys that can go for hundreds and thousands of dollars at auctions.

A collection of twig furniture, fishing collectibles, camp signs, nets, and other "goodies" occupy the corner of a 1930s log cabin in the Adirondacks.

Don't think that by saving a few dollars you're getting a deal. Believe me, there are very sophisticated and knowledgeable people out there and it isn't often anymore that people find a real bargain in the market. The reasons for this are many: popular TV shows that give antiques appraisals have educated many; there are more books available on the subjects; and the Internet is a ready source of information.

Keep in mind that you don't have to have 10,000 twig stands occupying every corner of your house to have a great collection. Buy the best you can find; make sure it is aesthetically pleasing, in excellent condition, and functional. That means if you are buying a chair, make sure it is comfortable before you purchase it.

When you are buying from any dealer, ask specific questions about the age and what has been done to the piece. Get as

This ornate frame, made from rhododendron branches in the early 1900s, was found at an auction in the Catskills region of New York.

A variation of the classic mosaic frame that originated in Europe.

much information as possible—and GET IT IN WRITING! I'm not kidding! If you're buying rustic furniture, keep in mind that it's very easy to cut down some dead branches, find some old barn boards, and use square nails to make a table. There are new copies of every object ever made presently on the market.

There is nothing wrong with contemporary things. There are many incredibly talented artists who are making wonderful objects of art. In my own collection I have several items from such artists as Barney Bellinger, Jack Leadley, Veronica Nemethy, and others. Just make sure you know whether the item is vintage or new so you don't get fooled by someone trying to pass off new work as antique.

Collections are never complete. Collecting is a lifelong endeavor that will enrich your life more than you realize.

This frame is nothing more than a hollowed-out burl taken from the side of a tree in the Adirondacks. It was finished in varnish that has mellowed to a dark brown.

A country farmhouse in New Hampshire is home to this impressive collection of hand-carved animal figures. Such figures are highly collectible. The Bedford Hickory Furniture Company made the dining-room chairs around the 1930s.

113

Collecting is better than therapy, Prozac, or anything else. Life is very short and nothing is more thrilling than a treasure hunt. We're talking about objects of art that have a profound history connected to them. It is absolutely thrilling to find something great!

One of the maxims in my life is that we have to continue to learn for as long as we are alive, and we have a responsibility to share that knowledge with others. That is one way the world becomes a better place. Write stuff down. When you learn something new, write it down. Your grandkids will thank you for the history you leave them.

I collect rustic stuff, and rustic stuff has an attitude. It is outside of

Decoupaging wooden slabs was a favorite project for youth groups around the country. Pictures were cut from magazines, glued to rough-cut wood slabs, and then varnished. Collections of these "curios" are inexpensive and fun to hunt, and they look great on wall displays.

Morey, Mich.

This small model of a two-story log cabin is made of dark maple sticks and was probably a young student's woodworking project. Many structures found today are quite fancy and were also built as birdhouses.

the mainstream of society. It goes against convention and is deeply rooted in our psyche. Rustic stuff is inherently fun, so do not take it seriously. You can be serious about Queen Anne highboys, Chippendale chests, impressionist paintings, Gustav Stickley sideboards, Jarvie candlesticks, Oriental rugs, Duncan Phyfe tables, and millions of other things, but not rustic stuff.

Rustic furniture insists that you relax. Forget about your job. Forget the business and your arrogant boss. Forget that you flunked algebra in high school. Forget everything. Just relax. Don't take anything seriously.

A classic late-Victorian frame covered with twig work.

Covered with hardwood burls cut from trees, this frame was found in Seattle.

Kick off your shoes. Listen to a few old Grateful Dead and Jefferson Airplane albums. Just think about hot summer days and a swimming hole. Remember fishing and boating and skiing and snowshoeing. Think of cool breezes and campfires. Think of elk and deer and birds and big trout jumping. Think of tall trees, cool water, and big mountains. Life is short so you need to think of good things, relaxing things. Rustic stuff lets you do that.

A small bedroom decorated in traditional rustic style features high-end snowshoes, creels, signs, paddles, pack baskets, and vintage canoes. The Rustic Hickory Furniture Company of La Porte, Indiana, made the bed around 1910.

Displays

There is an old adage that says "Presentation Is Everything." This is absolutely the truth.

There are two types of displays. The one that is closest to my heart is the chaotic/neurotic look, which fits my personality. I like lots of things everywhere and can never have enough. The other approach is more like my

A collection of "weird wood" items is displayed on a tea cart made in the 1930s by Adirondack builder Lee Fountain.

wife, who is much more talented and calm of nature than I. She prefers the plain and simple look. Since she worked in the design and window-display business for years, she likes order and structure and telling stories with each display.

The best form to look at when arranging displays is to consider the naturally occurring forms in nature. Mountains and many trees are big on the bottom and small on the top. Therefore, it makes sense that big picture frames go on the bottom and small ones on top. Also, if you put small items in front and large ones in back then you can see all the items. Don't forget to tell stories and utilize groupings with your treasures.

Not all rustic settings are log cabins. This home provides an ideal place to display a pair of very rare early-1900s bird's-eye maple canoe paddles. The center crest on the blades of both paddles is a classic coastal Native American design. Handmade creels, painted paddles, antique furniture from the Old Hickory Furniture Company, and other rustic items add to the ambiance.

An Old Hickory bookcase provides a setting for these rustic pieces. The items on the second shelf of the case, jokingly referred to as "weird wood," were traditionally made of ash and sold to the tourist trade. Pieces are often found with decals declaring such places as "The Adirondacks" or "The Catskills." It is not uncommon to find mugs, clocks, bowls, salt-and-pepper shakers, lamps, small chests, and other items made in this style.

A collection of "weird wood" accessories, which were always made from ash, can be found around the country. Many such items have decals from different regions of the country.

Resources

Where to Buy Stuff

Check out the auction pages of your local newspapers. Subscribe to any number of antique trade journals that are located throughout the country. Go early to antiques shows and pay the early buyer's fee to pre-view the sales before the general public is admitted. Visit your local antiques dealers and let them know what you're looking for. Check out the yard sales in the towns located near wilderness areas. Run ads looking for certain items. Work hard and have fun.

You may also wish to contact any of the following:

Sharon Boucher
Avalanche Ranch
12863 Hwy 133
Redstone, CO 81623
970-963-2846
877-963-2339 toll-free
970-963-3141 fax
aranch@rof.net
www.avalancheranch.com

Henry Caldwell
Black Bass Antiques
P.O. Box 778
Main Street
Bolton Landing, NY 12814
518-644-2389
518-644-2047 fax
hacantique@aol.com
www.blackbassantiques.com

Mark Catman
Birch Bark Designs
47 Main Street
East Berne, NY 12059
518-872-9614

Brian Correll
Correll Antiques
499 North Main
Gloversville, NY 12078
518-725-2049
518-725-5596 fax
bdcorr@klink.net

Thom Heil and
Paula Jenkins
Rustic Comforts
120 Main Street
Milford, Ohio 45150
513-965-8944 ph/fax
www.rusticcomforts.com

Bob Hoffman
Moose River Lake
and Lodge Store
370 Railroad Street
St. Johnsbury, VT 05819
802-748-2423
802-751-8598 fax

Ralph Kylloe Gallery
P.O. Box 669
Lake George, NY 12845
518-696-4100
rkylloe@capital.net
www.ralphkylloe.com

Jon and Carla Magoun
125 Ryerson Hill
South Paris, ME 04281
207-743-2040

Connie and Rich Moore
Country Road Antiques
4122 West Small Road
La Porte, IN 46350
219-362-5308

Bert Savage
Bert Savage–Larch Lodge
Route 126 Box 11
Center Strafford, NH 03815
603-269-7411

Bob Oestreicher
Moose America Antiques
97 Main Street
Rangeley, ME 04970
207-864-3699 ph/fax
603-431-9765 ph/fax
bobmemoose@mediaone.net

The Old Hickory
Furniture Company
403 South Noble Street
Shelbyville, IN 46176
317-392-6740
800-232-2275 toll-free
317-398-2275 fax
mail@oldhickory.com
www.oldhickory.com

Hank and Robert Ross
Ross Bros.
28 North Maple Street
Florence, MA 01062
413-586-3875
mail@rossbros.com
www.rossbros.com
603-269-2242 fax
rustic@worldpath.net

Terry and Sandy Winchell
Fighting Bear Antiques
PO Box 3790
375 South Cache Drive
Jackson, WY 83001
307-733-2669 ph/fax

Jim Worcester
PO Box 502
Antrim, NH 03440
603-588 3775

Resources

Books

Here are a few really good books:

The Art of the Creel
Blue Heron Publications
Box 1309
Ennis, MT 59729
888-BL-HERON

**The Bark Canoes and Skin
Boats of North America
Edwin Adney and
Howard Chapelle
Smithsonian Institution**
1000 Jefferson Drive S.W.
Washington, DC 20560
202-357-1300

**Birch Bark Canoe
David Gidmark
Firefly Books**
3680 Victoria Park Avenue
Willowdale, Ontario M2H3K1
Canada

**A History of the Old
Hickory Chair Company
Ralph Kylloe, Ed.D.**
P.O. Box 669
Lake George, NY 12845
518-696-4100

**Making the
Attikamek Snowshoe
Henri Vaillancourt**
Box 142
Greenville, NH 03048
603-878-2944